KUDOS for Pascha Press

"Their wonderful books easily guide children through the funeral process, while helping to instill a lifelong reverence for and understanding of the importance of funerals."

—Alexandra Kathryn Mosca,
   author of *Grave Undertakings* and *Green-Wood Cemetery*

"*When My Baba Died* and *When My Yiayia Died* are welcome resources for Orthodox caregivers facing the difficult task of tenderly guiding their children through the mourning process. The author, Marjorie Kunch, writes gently and straightforwardly about what to expect at an Orthodox funeral service and the array of emotions attached to grief. Kids and adults alike will greatly benefit from these unique tools for teaching Orthodox Christians of all ages about the Church's hope-filled response to death and eternity."

—Molly Sabourin,
   author of *Close to Home: One Orthodox Mother's Quest for Patience, Peace and Perseverance*

WHEN MY YIAYIA DIED

When My Yiayia Died

Marjorie Kunch

FOREWORD BY FATHER KONSTANTINOS TSIOLAS

Although you feel thorns of grief at your family member's passing,
know their love will forever bloom within your heart
like an unfading rose.

PASCHA PRESS

Educate   Edify   Entertain

Pascha Press
http://www.paschapress.com

Toll-free telephone: 1-844-4-PASCHA

Email: mkunch@paschapress.com

This publication is designed to provide accurate information, for general purposes only, in regard to the subject matter covered. There are no warranties or representations, expressed or implied. It is sold with the understanding that the publisher and author are not engaged in rendering legal, medical, or other professional services. If legal advice or other expert assistance is required, the services of a competent professional person should be sought.

ISBN 978-0-9964045-4-9

Library of Congress Control Number: 2017902632

Dedicated to all who by loving deeply, have grieved deeply.
Many thanks to my loving family and devoted friends,
I am forever grateful.
Thank you to Bishop Damasceno, Father Milos, Father Kosta,
and all the priests and monastics
who have assisted my journey to Orthodoxy,
my funeral service colleagues,
and to those instrumental in the production of this book
by word, deed, or prayer:
Christopher, Everilde, Mattias;
also Alexander, Faye, Irina, James, Jane, Jose,
Kim, Megan, Michelle, Mike, Nikki, Pam, Ray,
and the parishioners of Saint Archangel Michael Serbian Orthodox Church.
Especially my namesake, my firecracker, my lilac blossom,
my Grammie.

ты ушёл от нас, но ты всегда в наших сердцах

Credits

Creative Director: Stephen Tiano

Editing: Bishop Damasceno Ribeiro and Pamela Cain Gonzalez

Images: Megan Duncan of Tricycle Motor Photography, Valparaiso, IN

      Alexander Ziemak of A2Z Photography, Hobart, IN

         http://www.a2zphoto.photo/ http://www.facebook.com/A2ZPhotographyNWI/

Software: Fotosketcher, Photoshop

Shot on location:

Bocken Funeral Home

Jose Corona-Owner

7042 Kennedy Avenue

Hammond, Indiana 46323

http://www.bockenfunerals.com

Elmwood Cemetery

Michael Gozdecki-Owner

1413 169th Street

Hammond, Indiana 46324

http://www.elmwoodcaskets.com

Saint Archangel Michael Serbian Orthodox Church

Very Reverend Father Milos Vesin-Pastor

1500 186th Street

Lansing, Illinois 60438

http://www.starchangelmichael.com

Icons:

Pg. 16-"Entombment of Christ" Russian, circa 1900 and "Virgin Mary Iverskaya" Russian, 17th C.

Pg. 17-"Anastasis" Greek, 11th C.

Clip art used with permission by ofc.org and sourced from the public domain.

In Memoriam

Thomas and Marjorie Burton

Wilma Eberly

Richard Heroux

Pauline Hettinger

Florence Shirley Kunch

Florence Medley

Raymond and Doris Neumeier

Madge Reardon

Julia Stillmack

Nancy Neumeier-West

Alec and Austin and all the Angel Babies in my life

Richard Bridegroom

Marilyn Cody

Curtis DeVries

Nancy Feldman

Vladyka Nicholas of Amissos

Steve and Laura Popiela

Steven J. Struck

Steve and Lorraine Vaclavik

Your loved ones, dear reader

FOREWORD

The passing of a loved one is a difficult event for many of us. Preparations for the funeral and the service itself can stir up many emotions, thoughts, and memories, all in the period of just a few days. The grieving process begins almost immediately and it can take a long time. This can be an especially confusing time for children, who can experience the same thoughts and feelings as adults, but often without the emotional maturity to understand, process, or verbalize their emotions. Death can be a difficult topic, but it can also be a way to help our children in their spiritual and emotional formation through the guidance of their parents, their priest, and the Church.

This book is a useful resource for parents, offering topics they can discuss with their children as they try to process the concept of death and loss. It is important to get children to talk about their thoughts and emotions during such a difficult event. Funeral preparations can be hectic, and children often become confused spectators during this time. Their routines are put aside for something special that they cannot fully understand. They know it is a sad occasion. They feel upset that their loved one has died and that people around them are upset and crying. They can also be confused about everything, from the funeral services, to the concept of death itself. We can help our children through the grieving process by listening to them and speaking with them with honesty and love. It is also quite important to give our children the understanding that our loved ones are still members of our family and of the Body of Christ, even after death.

Sometimes as parents we don't feel comfortable discussing such heavy and deep subjects with our children. To shelter our children from the reality of death is not the answer, as it is something that we will experience one day. It is up to us to give our children the Orthodox understanding of the meaning of death, not as a defeat and an end, but as Christ's victory on the Cross. It is a chance for us to teach our children about the Resurrection of Christ and His promise of eternal life in His Kingdom.

Rev. Konstantinos Tsiolas
St. Demetrios Greek Orthodox Church
Winnipeg, Canada

TABLE OF CONTENTS

✠ 13 ✠

One winter day, Mama and Papa shared sad news. My Yiayia died. Her soul was called home by God so now her body and mind no longer work. I wondered; was I bad, did I make her die somehow? I felt sad, scared, and mad. These feelings in my heart are called **grief**. Do you feel grief because your loved one died, too?

Mama said it was ok to cry and feel grief. Even Jesus wept when His friend died. Papa explained that although Yiayia may be gone from this life, she lives in the next. We will still pray for her when we stand in our icon corner. Nothing I did made her die. It was just time for her soul to join the **Church Triumphant**. That is what we call the people who died and live with God now. The angels rejoiced when Yiayia arrived at her heavenly home. Her parents awaited their reunion, even her Yiayia will be there!

My Yiayia is happy and safe with God. Together they are in a place of peace and light where tears do not exist. She is no longer sick or in pain. You may hear the priest say your loved one "fell asleep" in the Lord. It is entirely different than falling asleep at bedtime. That is just when my body rests and I awaken to a new day. To die is to have your soul rest and then awaken to the perpetual joy of eternal day. Imagine, **Pascha**, in heaven!

Now we know a little bit about Yiayia's spirit, what about her body? What do we do to say goodbye to her here on earth, what do we do to help our grief? Are you curious to know what my family did next?

PART ONE

THE VISITATION AND TRISAGION

Christ is risen, and the angels rejoice!
Christ is risen, and life reigns!
 —Paschal homily
  St. John Chrystostom

First, the **priest** was called and he began praying for Yiayia to help her spirit's journey. Next, Mama and Papa met with a person called a **funeral director** to help plan her service. The **funeral** is a ceremony where we say goodbye to our loved one.

Father and the funeral director will help take good care of Yiayia's soul and body. They will help take good care of my family. Do you think priests and funeral directors are important helpers?

Next, Mama and Papa took me to the **funeral home**. This is a building where people who died go to get ready for their ceremony. The funeral home is large so that everyone can come visit, or pay their respects, to Yiayia. Inside it was cozy and familiar, just like my living room at home. Families can also choose to have the visitation in their church instead of the funeral home. They can choose whichever is most comforting for them and the funeral director will make it so. I saw Yiayia in her **casket**. She was still, her eyes were closed, and her hands were folded on her tummy. Yiayia looked peaceful just as she was. Sometimes the professional services of a person called an **embalmer** is called upon to help loved ones look like themselves again after a long illness.

Marjorie Kunch

A casket is the name of the pretty box she was in. These boxes are made of either wood or metal. I could not see Yiayia's feet, but I knew that they were there. Her entire body is precious and so we treat it with respect. I showed respect by being on my best behavior.

Everyone came to the funeral home to talk, cry, and share happy memories of Yiayia at her **visitation**. Yes, adults cry too and that is ok. What joyful memories do you have of your loved one? Everyone feels better when they talk about them.

✝ 22 ✝

The priest came to sing the memorial, or **Trisagion**, prayers. He talked about Jesus and heaven. This made me feel comforted. I felt sad Yiayia died but I do believe that I will see her again one day. Jesus said so. He promised everyone eternal life if they believe in Him. Yiayia believed in The Father, the Son, and the Holy Spirit and so do I.

The priest also spoke nicely about Yiayia at her **eulogy**, or speech, about her life. When the viewing ended we lined up to kiss an icon of the Resurrection, placed at the corner of her casket. Then the grown-ups gathered to drink coffee and share a bit of brandy. I had cookies called **Paximadia**. We went home but we will see Yiayia again in the morning. Want to know what happened next?

✝ 23 ✝

PART TWO

THE FUNERAL CEREMONY

With the saints give rest, O Christ,
to the soul of Thy servant,
where there is neither sickness,
nor sorrow, nor sighing,
but life everlasting.
　　　　　　–Eastern Orthodox
　　　　　　Memorial Service

The day after the visitation, my family gathered at church for Yiayia's funeral. Early morning sunlight streamed in the windows and the candlelight danced, everything was radiant.

We stood in the **narthex**, or entrance, to the church and **venerated**, or kissed, the icons. Mama brought **sitari**. I held a candle. Yiayia got to hold something, too.

We took our places inside the church and the funeral service began.

Yiayia's casket was opened and the priest placed his hand cross and an icon on the corner. These items showed she belonged to the Holy Orthodox Church. Our prayers helped her soul be at peace.

The priest walked around Yiayia's casket and everybody in attendance with a **censer**. The smoke symbolizes our prayers rising to heaven. Do you think **incense** smells like Nativity, or perhaps roses? Does it make you want to sneeze?

The priest stood in the center of church and recited sacred prayers. He then went to the **Royal Gate** and read from the Holy Gospel. Father spoke about the Resurrection of Christ and our own future resurrection. Everyone listened carefully and let these words into their hearts. It helped our grief not feel so bad.

*Sprinkle me with hyssop and I shall be cleansed, wash me
and I shall be whiter than snow.*—Psalm 51:7

Father then put a mixture of wine
and oil on Yiayia's forehead to
remind us of her baptism and bless
her body. Did you know the priest
anointed your body with **holy oil**
when you were baptized? Every
Orthodox person in the world had
this anointing done to them, too.

Everyone in church walked by Yiayia's casket for one last kiss. I felt a little scared to lean in and kiss her while she lay inside of the casket, but Mama helped me. I was surprised that Yiayia felt cold, but this is because the warmth of her spirit has left her body.

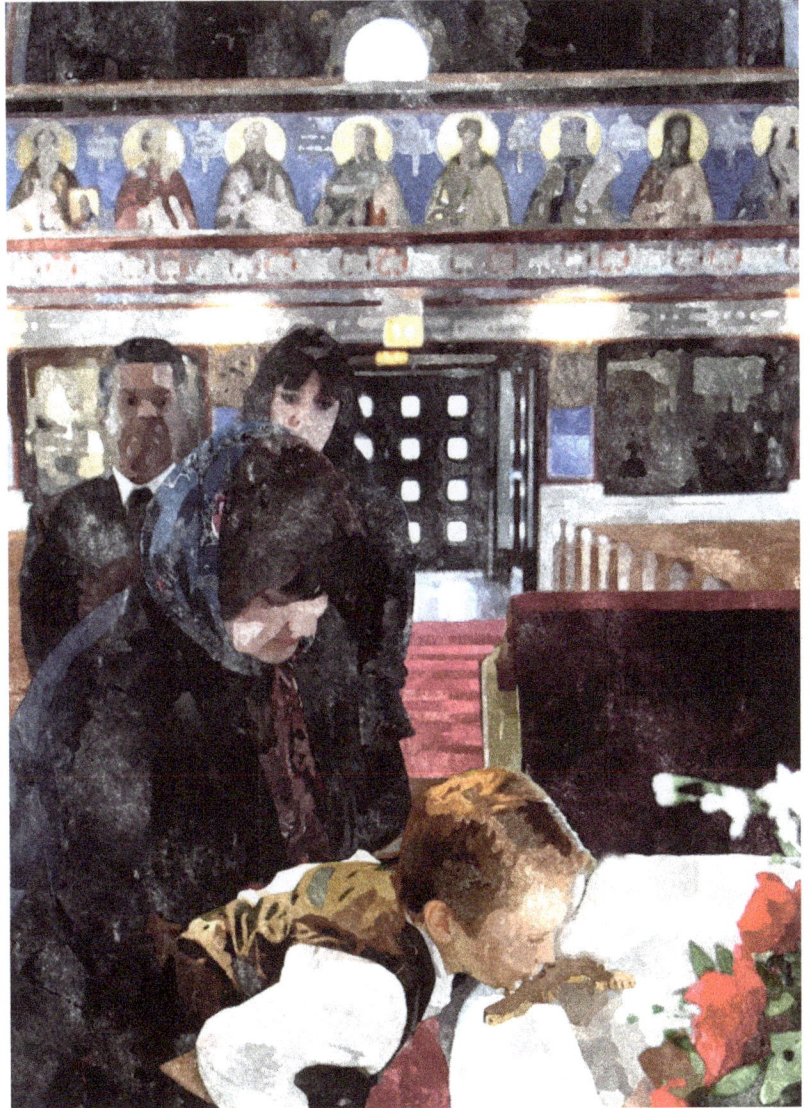

I silently asked God and the **Theotokos** to help me be brave. The Blessed Virgin Mary once had to kiss her Son goodbye at His funeral, too.

I knew I would not see Yiayia again in this life except in pictures and memories so it was important I gave her that final gift. I am so glad I did.

Now we were almost done. The priest brought my family the golden cross to kiss.

Do you remember the term for when we kiss something in church?

Father blessed Yiayia one last time by making the sign of the cross, then her casket was closed.

The funeral director wheeled Yiayia's casket down the aisle. Sometimes six people are chosen from the family to help with the casket, this honor is called being a **pallbearer**. Father sang while he led everyone out of church.

Yiayia was then put in a **hearse**, a special shiny car built to carry caskets. We took one last trip with her and drove to the cemetery.

This line of cars traveling behind the hearse is called a **funeral procession**.

✝ 35 ✝

PART THREE

THE COMMITTAL SERVICE

Christ is risen, and not one dead
remains in the grave.
For Christ, being risen from the dead,
is become the first fruits of those
who have fallen asleep.
　　　—Paschal homily
　　　St. John Chrystostom

Do you wonder what a **cemetery** is like? This is where people who died are kept. Cemeteries are restful places, like a park or garden. There are graceful trees, colorful flowers, some even have carved marble statues and bubbling water fountains. Mama said I did not have to worry about seeing dead bodies there like in the scary stories bigger kids tell. That is just make-believe.

The people who died are tucked inside their **interred** caskets, another way of saying "put away." I did see **headstones** and **plaques**, these mark where other people's loved ones are. I thought I would be afraid, but it turns out I liked visiting Yiayia's place in the cemetery. It's not spooky at all. Visiting someone's **grave** is a way to show love. Every time we go to the cemetery, I look around and give thanks for all of God's creation: birds, flowers, trees, and Yiayia.

At the cemetery, helpers moved Yiayia's casket from the hearse to her grave. Sometimes caskets are buried underground in a strong, protective box called a **vault**. Sometimes caskets are placed in a **crypt** at the **mausoleum**, an above ground building. Even Jesus had His earthly body placed in a tomb and that is why Orthodox Christians are always interred.

"Thou art earth and to earth shalt thou return ... "

The priest chanted more prayers. He took sand and poured a cross on the casket. This **consecrated**, or made holy, her grave. The cemetery workers came and interred Yiayia's casket. This is where Yiayia's body will stay, alongside the graves of her parents and even her Yiayia. Although someone has died, they will always remain a part of our family. Before everyone left, we sang "Memory Eternal" together. *Eonia I Mnimi!*

This concluded the funeral service, but it did not conclude our remembering, our sharing, or our love for Yiayia. When we left the cemetery, my family hosted a luncheon called a **Makaria** as a way to say "thank you" to everyone who attended her services.

My family went back to church forty days after Yiayia's funeral and celebrated a special service called the **Mnimosino**. We remember her and all of our **ancestors** throughout the year. These are important traditions that help us honor their memory.

As winter melts into spring, so too will our grief eventually melt into warm remembrance. My family visited Yiayia's grave often and when May arrived, I planted fragrant pink hydrangeas by her headstone. They were her favorite. The seasons of life, the seasons of Church, the seasons of nature, everything points to our Creator and His love for us.

My Yiayia, and all of the Orthodox faithful who have passed away, are forever remembered during **Soul Saturdays**. It makes me happy to hear the priest say her name and to hear everyone in church pray for her.

I give thanks to God for gifting us with wonderful traditions to live by and an eternal home in heaven to live for. I give thanks to God for blessing me with such lovely memories of Yiayia. I give thanks to God for all of the helpers.

When my Yiayia died, I learned about all the different ways people can help. Although I am little, even I am a helper, because I pray for Yiayia. Are you a helper, too?

GLOSSARY OF TERMS

Ancestor A person from whom one is descended. Your grandparents are an example, the grandparents of your grandparents, and so on.

Casket Originally meaning a small ornamental box for holding jewels or other valuable objects, it is now the term which replaces "coffin" and is the container a deceased person is laid within.

Cemetery A burial ground, a graveyard, a place set aside for the burial or interment of people who have died. Taken from the Greek word *koimeterion* meaning the "sleeping place".

Censer A ceramic or metal container in which incense is burned during a religious ceremony.

Church Triumphant Members of the Orthodox Church who have died and are now enjoying eternal happiness through union with God and the saints in heaven.

Consecrate To declare or set someone, something, or someplace apart as belonging to God.

Crypt A room or vault which is used for the burial of people who have died, also known as a tomb.

Embalmer A professional man or woman who uses both art and science to prepare the deceased for their visitation.

Eulogy A speech in honor of a deceased person telling of their life and all of the good things they had done.

Funeral The ceremonies honoring a deceased person, held a few days after death and prior to their burial.

Funeral Director A professional man or woman involved in the planning, preparation, and arrangement of funeral ceremonies. Also known as a mortician or an undertaker.

Funeral Home   An establishment where people who have died are prepared for funeral ceremonies and where the living gather to pay their respects. Also known as a funeral parlor, life celebration center, or mortuary.

Funeral Procession   A group of cars which travels behind a hearse en route to the cemetery, also called a funeral cortege. In some pious communities, it is customary for mourners to leave their cars upon entering the cemetery and walk behind the hearse to the grave.

Grave   A hole dug in the earth in which to bury a deceased person.

Grief   The normal process of reacting to a profound loss; a feeling of deep sorrow.

Headstone   A slab of stone set above a grave, typically engraved with the deceased's name and dates of birth and death. A memorial stone or monument.

Hearse   A special vehicle built to drive a casket where the funeral ceremony and burial will take place.

Holy Oil   The portion of olive oil that was blessed by a priest when celebrating Holy Unction for the sick and is reserved for funerals. Oftentimes it is mixed with wine, to remind us of the parable of the Good Samaritan.

Incense   A gum, resin, or spice which releases a sweet smell when burned upon a lit charcoal.

Inter   The act of putting a casket away inside of a crypt, grave, or tomb.

Makaria   A meal which all mourners are invited to partake following the graveside service. Traditionally in the Greek Orthodox Church, the main dish is broiled fish. This is because the first meal that the Lord Jesus ate with His disciples following His resurrection from the dead consisted of broiled fish and bread, as recorded in the *Gospel of John 21:12-13*. This meal is a reminder of Christ's resurrection and His closeness to those who believe in Him.

Mausoleum   A place that houses crypts or tombs, either privately for a family or a large, stately stone building constructed for many people.

Mnimosino   The "Calling to Mind" service is done in remembrance of a loved one. These prayers are most commonly added to the Divine Liturgy on Sundays. Family and friends of the deceased sit in reserved seats in the front of the church. It is offered so that the deceased may receive mercy and forgiveness for the sins they may have committed in their lives. Christ, the Theotokos, and the saints are asked to intercede on behalf of the departed.

Narthex   The porch or vestibule, the western entrance to an Orthodox Church.

Pallbearer   One of six people chosen to help assist with a casket, usually the next of kin of or special friends to the deceased.

Pascha   The great and joyous Feast of the Resurrection of Our Lord, the Easter holiday.

Paximadia   Or *paximathia*, a hard biscotti-like bread of Greek origin that is prepared with barley flour, chick peas, or whole wheat.

Plaque   An ornamental tablet fixed to a wall, usually to mark a crypt or tomb. The equivalent of a headstone over a grave.

Priest   A man called specially by God to serve His people. Ranking below a bishop but above a deacon, he has authority to administer the Holy Mysteries such as baptism, confession, marriage, and funerals.

Resurrection   The most fundamental belief of the Church, Christ died and after three days in the tomb, He arose. This Truth is celebrated every Pascha and it is what the Orthodox faithful have to look forward to after their death, arising with Christ in the never ending day of eternal joy.

Royal Gate   Also known as the royal doors, holy doors, or beautiful gates, These are the central doors of the iconostasis found in an Eastern Orthodox Christian church.

Sitari   A dish of boiled wheat, honey, raisins, and other sweet dried fruit. It is brought to Orthodox funerals and memorial services for blessing and sharing with all who attend. It symbolizes the resurrection in reference to *John 12:24* and reminds us of the joyfulness and sweetness of the Heavenly Kingdom. Also known as koliva.

Soul Saturday   Days set aside for commemoration of the dead within the liturgical year of the Eastern Orthodox Church. Saturday is a traditional day for prayer for the dead, because Christ lay dead in the tomb on Saturday.

Theotokos   The Greek name for the Mother of our Lord and God Jesus Christ, the Ever-Virgin Mary. *Theo* = God, *Tokos* = the one who gave birth to.

Tomb   An above ground burial chamber in which caskets are placed.

Trisagion Τρισάγιον "Thrice Holy", sometimes called by its opening line "*Agios Theos*". A memorial service chanted for the repose of the deceased. Also called a *Parastos*, *Panikhida*, or *Pomen*. It consists of Psalms, litanies, hymns, and prayers.

Vault A container made of concrete and steel that caskets are placed within for underground burial.

Venerate To regard with high respect. To respectfully bow, make the sign of the cross, and kiss a holy icon as a sign of piety and devotion. Not to be confused with worship, which belongs to God alone.

Visitation Also called a wake, viewing, or calling hours, a custom where family and friends come to pay respects to the deceased and show support for the surviving kin.

Rev. Fr. Konstantinos Tsiolas was born in Kastoria, Macedonia, Greece. Fr. Kosta was a founding member and counsellor of Camp Metamorphosis in Toronto, Canada. It is here he realized his passion for working with young people and how much he enjoyed youth ministry. He attended the Toronto Orthodox Theological Academy from 1999 to 2002. Fr. Kosta and his family, formerly of Ontario and BC, moved to St. Demetrios Greek Orthodox Church of Winnipeg in 2014, to serve the church and the spiritual needs of the faithful of Manitoba.

Marjorie Kunch is a mother, mortician, and Orthodox Christian who traded the snowy Midwest for the sunny Southwest. Marjorie and her husband converted to Orthodoxy on Holy Saturday 2005. She graduated Magna Cum Laude from Worsham College of Mortuary Science in 2003 and currently serves her community as a Certified Funeral Celebrant.

Blessed are they whom Thou hast chosen and taken, O Lord,
their memory is from generation to generation,
their souls shall dwell with the blessed.
Alleluia! Alleluia! Alleluia!

ALSO AVAILABLE FROM PASCHA PRESS

ACTIVITY WORKBOOK *for When My Baba ♥ My Yiayia Died*

This companion full-color workbook provides meaningful ways to help children participate in saying goodbye to an Orthodox Christian loved one. It also includes reinforcement of concepts presented such as vocabulary review and word searches, open ended questions and journaling space to help a child process their emotions, coloring pages, an icon to keep, the recipe for a traditional Orthodox funeral food children can help prepare, and Bible verses to look up and discuss. Perfect for both grieving families to complete together or as a tool in the classroom to discuss the inevitable experience of death and the Orthodox response to it. Also useful for students of our multicultural society studying religions of the world or holding an interest in funeral rites and customs.

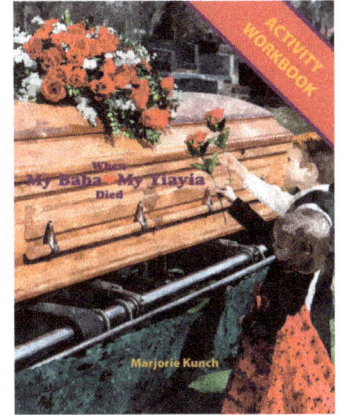

Written by a funeral director and Certified Funeral Celebrant who has served thousands of families over twelve years, this title honors Church Tradition, introduces children to Greek and Slavic cultural heritage, and evolving funerary practices.

Find this title on any retail bookseller website, ask your church bookstore to order, or contact the publisher directly:

PASCHA PRESS

Educate   Edify   Entertain

www.paschapress.com
mkunch@paschapress.com
1-844-4-PASCHA

www.ingramcontent.com/pod-product-compliance
Lightning Source LLC
Chambersburg PA
CBHW040302100426
42811CB00011B/1341